MY FIRST WORDS

Book for Kids

26 Pages and 8,5x8,5 in

VEGETABLES

FRUITS

FOOD

DRINKS

PETS

CLOTHES

MUSIC INSTRUMENTS

VEGETABLES

AUBERGINE

POTATO

CARROT

RADISH

LEEK

BROCCOLI

CAULIFLOWER

PEA

MUSHROOM

COURGETTE

TOMATO

ONION

CORN

PEPPER

FRUITS

WATERMELON

PEARS

STRAWBERRY

CHERRY

GRAPES

MANGO

PINEAPPLE

PEACH

MANDARINE

APPLE

BANANA

LEMON

BLACKBERRY

ORANGE

FOOD

PIZZA

SANDWICH

FRITTES

HAMBURGER

SALAD

STEAK

Chicken
NUGGETS

PANCAKE

TACOS

YOGURT

TOAST

EGG

BREAD

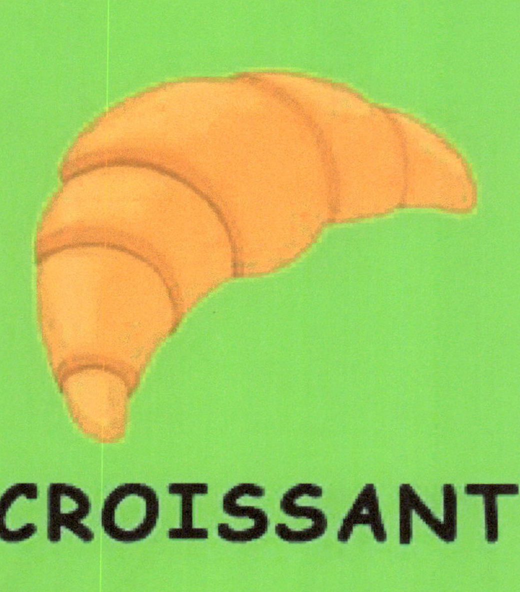

CROISSANT

CHEESE

DRINKS

COFFEE

JUICE

TEA

MILKSHAKE

LEMONADE

PETS

CAT

DOG

HAMSTER

PARROT

MOUSE

PIGEON

TURTLE

RABBIT

CHIKEN

CLOTHES

SHIRT

JEAN

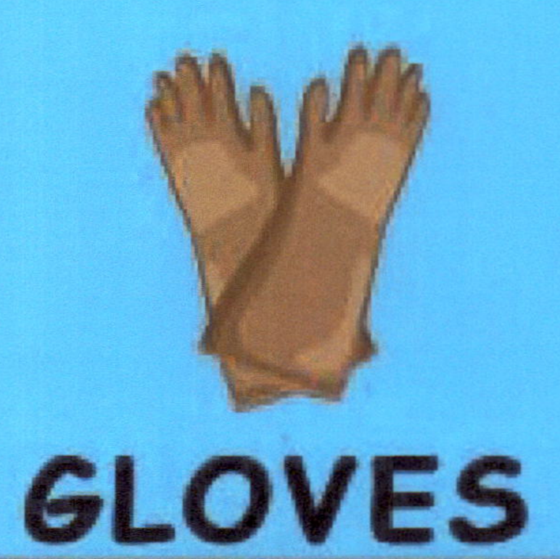

GLOVES

SUIT

CAP

SHOE

JACKET

SLIPPERS

SOCKS

SHORT

SCARF

BELT

TIE

GLASSES

MUSIC INSTRUMENTS

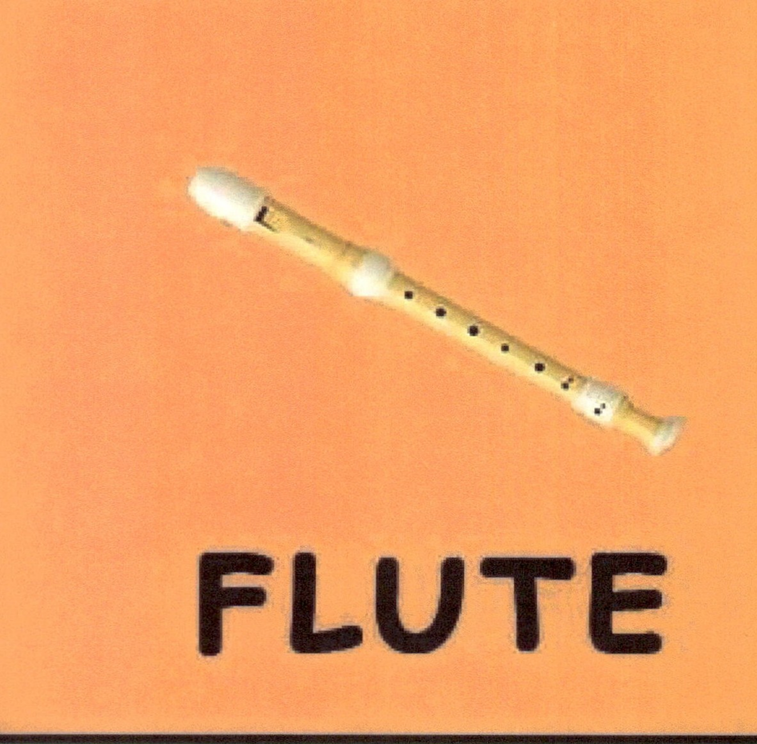
FLUTE

ACCORDION

PIANO

GUITAR

BANJO

HARP

DRUMS

VIOLIN

SAXOPHONE

www.ingramcontent.com/pod-product-compliance
Lightning Source LLC
Chambersburg PA
CBHW040037240726

48664CB00003B/968